SUCCESSFUL AMERICANS

Chinese Americans

Jack Adler

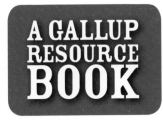

A GALLUP
RESOURCE
BOOK

Mason Crest Publishers
Philadelphia

Produced by OTTN Publishing in association with
Bow Publications, Inc.

MASON CREST PUBLISHERS INC.
370 Reed Road
Broomall, Pennsylvania 19008
(866) MCP-BOOK (toll free)
www.masoncrest.com

Printed in the United States of America.

First Printing

9 8 7 6 5 4 3 2 1

Library of Congress Cataloging-in-Publication Data

Adler, Jack.
  Chinese Americans / Jack W. Adler.
      p. cm. — (Successful Americans)
  Includes bibliographical references and index.
  ISBN-13: 978-1-4222-0520-4 (hardcover)
  ISBN-13: 978-1-4222-0855-7 (pbk.)
  1. Chinese Americans—Biography—Juvenile literature. 2. Successful people—
United States—Biography—Juvenile literature. I. Title.
  E184.C5A35 2008
  920'.0092951073—dc22
                                                              2008029810

Publisher's note:
All quotations in this book come from original sources, and contain the spelling
and grammatical inconsistencies of the original text.

◀ **CROSS-CURRENTS** ▶

When you see this logo, turn
to the Cross-Currents section
at the back of the book. The
Cross-Currents features explore
connections between people,
places, events, and ideas.

Table of Contents

CHAPTER 1   Chinese-American Immigration   5

CHAPTER 2   I. M. Pei: Architect   12

CHAPTER 3   Daniel C. Tsui: Physicist   18

CHAPTER 4   Laurence Yep: Storyteller   23

CHAPTER 5   Amy Tan: Author   28

CHAPTER 6   Elaine Chao: U.S. Secretary of Labor   33

CHAPTER 7   Yo-Yo Ma: Musician   39

CHAPTER 8   Lucy Liu: Actress   45

CROSS-CURRENTS   51

NOTES   56

GLOSSARY   58

FURTHER READING   59

INTERNET RESOURCES   59

OTHER SUCCESSFUL CHINESE AMERICANS   60

INDEX   62

Beginning in the late 1800s, Chinese immigrants formed communities that were known as Chinatowns in cities across North America.

CHAPTER ONE

Chinese-American Immigration

According to a 2006 survey by the U.S. Census Bureau, approximately 13 million people in the United States report that they are of Asian ancestry. That is, they or their ancestors came from the Far East, Southeast Asia, or the Indian subcontinent. Almost a quarter of that population—or approximately 2.9 million—originated in China.

People of Chinese ancestry come from a vast area that includes mainland China (the People's Republic of China), its administrative regions of Hong Kong and Macau, and the nation of Taiwan (the Republic of China). They may speak one or more of the major dialects of the Chinese language, including Mandarin, Shanghainese, Cantonese, and Min.

EARLY CHINESE IMMIGRATION

The year 1849 marked the beginning of major Chinese immigration to the United States. Gold had been discovered in California, and the hope of making a fortune in what was known as *Gam Sann*, or "Gold Mountain," drew many poor Chinese immigrants. Most were farmers from the Guangdong Province of southern China, where floods and crop failures had brought poverty and famine.

As of 1851 fewer than 3,000 Chinese men were living in the United States. By the end of the following year, that figure had increased to more than 20,000. Many of the new immigrants came to the United States with the goal of making money and returning home with great wealth. A few were so fortunate; most were not.

The Chinese newcomers faced widespread discrimination. Laws in California were passed that limited the jobs they could have and barred them from owning land or filing mining claims. During the mid-1850s it became illegal for a Chinese immigrant to testify in court against whites.

Forced out of the gold fields, the Chinese had to look for other ways to make a living. Some found work as migrant workers, in fisheries, or in factories making shoes and sewing clothes. Some Chinese immigrants opened their own shops or laundries in the growing mining towns of California.

Despite these difficulties, the wave of emigration from China continued. In 1860 there were over 100,000 Chinese-Americans in the United States. Most lived in California and the western regions of the country. During the 1860s more than 10,000 of them were recruited to help build the western section of the first transcontinental railroad. Workers helped lay tracks for the Central Pacific Railroad, which ran from Sacramento eastward through the Sierra Nevada mountain range.

CHINESE EXCLUSION ACTS

By 1882 an estimated 110,000 Chinese were living in the United States. As the number of Chinese increased, so did incidents of discrimination. That year the U.S. Congress passed the first of the Chinese Exclusion Acts. The act prevented Chinese resident aliens—people already living in the country—from becoming U.S. citizens. The Chinese Exclusion Act of 1882 also barred most immigration from China for ten years.

The majority of Chinese immigrants were men. The law meant they could not bring their wives and families over from China. Unmarried Chinese men were expected to marry Chinese women, but there were few of them. One 1880 California

population estimate indicated there were 70,000 Chinese men but fewer than 4,000 Chinese women.

A decade later, the law was renewed, and the following decade, in 1902, it was made permanent. As a result of immigration restrictions, the Chinese community did not grow, and most immigrants did not assimilate into U.S. society.

From 1860 to 1865 more than 10,000 Chinese laborers helped build the transcontinental railroad for the Central Pacific Railroad.

GROWTH OF BENEVOLENT ASSOCIATIONS

Starting in the 1870s, many Chinese immigrants began to form community associations to help out other immigrants coming from the same regions of China. These benevolent and business associations helped newcomers find jobs and helped care for the sick and poor.

Local associations also helped govern the Chinese communities, or Chinatowns, that developed in major urban areas. Large communities formed in cities such as San Diego and San

Chinese-American Immigration

Francisco, California, and Vancouver, British Columbia, Canada. By the early 1900s, there were Chinatowns in cities across North America—including New York City; Detroit, Michigan; and Chicago, Illinois.

LEGAL IMMIGRATION

Despite the obstacles, there was some legal immigration. In 1910, a facility at Angel Island, near San Francisco, opened to serve as an entry point for immigrants who came mostly from China. Over the next 30 years, officials at the Angel Island Immigration Station would detain immigrants, usually for two- to three-week periods. During that time the new arrivals would be interrogated to see whether they could prove they were citizens of the United States.

By law, the children of immigrants are citizens of the United States if born in the United States. So, if a Chinese immigrant

From 1910 to 1940 the Angel Island immigration station, near San Francisco, California, detained and processed thousands of people hoping to enter the United States from Asia.

could prove that his or her father was a citizen of the United States, that person was legally allowed to enter the United States. About 175,000 Chinese immigrants would pass through Angel Island between 1910 and 1940.

CHANGES IN IMMIGRATION LAW

After dropping to a low of around 61,000 in 1920, the Chinese population in the United States began to increase again. After China became the U.S. ally in the fight against Japan during World War II (1940–1945), Americans became more sympathetic to Chinese-Americans. In 1943 the Chinese Exclusion Act was repealed. Thousands of Chinese aliens in the United States became eligible for citizenship, making them the first group of immigrants from Asia to receive the right to seek naturalization. However, Chinese immigration was still restricted. Only 105 Chinese immigrants were allowed to enter the country per year.

During the 1940s there was civil war in China. The Nationalists, led by Chiang Kai-shek, were fighting the Communists,

◀ CROSS-CURRENTS ▶

To see how Americans feel about overall immigration to the United States, turn to page 51.

led by Mao Zedong. By 1949 the Nationalists had fled to Taiwan. The Chinese Communist Party took control of the mainland, where it established the People's Republic of China. The new Communist government did not allow immigration to the United States, and the U.S. government cut all diplomatic ties.

A RISE IN CHINESE IMMIGRATION

In 1965 a new U.S. immigration law did away with "national origins" as the basis for allocating immigration quotas. The Immigration and Naturalization Act of 1965 permitted 20,000 immigrants each year, not including wives who desired to join

U.S. ATTITUDES TOWARD CHINA, 1980-2008

Through the years Gallup polls have measured Americans' attitudes toward the People's Republic of China. Since the 1990s, the overall opinion has been negative.

What is your overall opinion of China—is it very favorable, mostly favorable, mostly unfavorable, or very unfavorable?

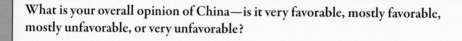

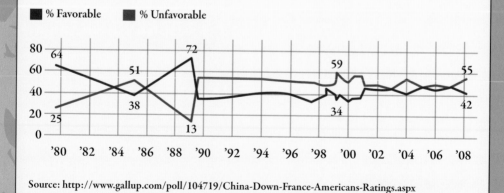

Source: http://www.gallup.com/poll/104719/China-Down-France-Americans-Ratings.aspx

their husbands and children who wanted to rejoin their parents. Ten years later, as a result of this new law, the Chinese-American population in the United States had almost doubled. By 1990 about 1.5 million U.S residents reported they were of Chinese ancestry. And in 2000, that number had increased to almost 2.3 million.

The following chapters contain biographies of contemporary Chinese Americans who have come to the United States or who are descended from earlier immigrants to America. All have made important contributions to the United States and helped add to the country's growth and prosperity.

CHAPTER TWO

I. M. Pei: Architect

Chinese-born I. M. Pei has made a name for himself as one of the world's leading architects. Known as a master of conservative modernistic architecture, Pei has been involved in the construction of more than 150 award-winning structures and complexes around the world.

LIFE IN CHINA

Ieoh Ming Pei was born on April 26, 1917, in Guangzhou (formerly known as Canton), which is in the southern part of today's People's Republic of China. In Chinese his name means "to inscribe brightly."

Ieoh Ming was born into a wealthy and prominent family. His father, Tsuyee Pei, was a well-to-do banker and his mother, Lien Kwun, was a poetess and flutist. The Pei family later moved to Hong Kong and in the late 1920s to Shanghai, where Ieoh Ming attended St. John's University. He had already learned English when he came to the United States to further his education.

A U.S. EDUCATION

In 1935 Pei arrived in the United States to study architecture. While a student at Massachusetts Institute of Technology (MIT), in Cambridge, Massachusetts, he began to use the initials I. M. in place of his full name. Five years later Pei received his bachelor of arts degree in architecture from MIT. He graduated with several honors, receiving the Alpha Ro Chi (fraternity of architects)

Medal, the MIT Traveling Fellowship, and the American Institute of Architects Gold Medal.

In 1942 Pei enrolled at the Harvard Graduate School of Design, also in Cambridge. That same year he married Eileen Loo, a Chinese student who had recently graduated from Wellesley College, in Wellesley, Massachusetts.

Studies at Harvard were interrupted with the advent of World War II. In 1943 Pei volunteered for a unit of the National Defense Research Committee, based in Princeton, New Jersey. The organization brought together civilian scientists to aid the war effort by doing military research. Pei worked on developing a fusing device for incendiary weapons.

In 1946 Pei completed his master's degree at the School of Design. After graduation, he remained at Harvard, where he served as an assistant professor. While teaching, he also worked in the office of architect Hugh Stubbins.

In this 1983 photograph I. M. Pei stands before the newly completed Weisner Building located on the campus of his alma mater— the Massachusetts Institute of Technology.

FROM PROFESSOR TO ARCHITECT

Pei's career path changed in 1948 when he accepted a position as director of architecture for the New York-based firm of Webb and Knapp, a real estate development corporation. His work with this prominent company on many large-scale projects gave him experience in corporate architecture: working with big budgets and with various community, business, and government agencies.

In 1955, a year after becoming an American citizen, Pei launched his own architectural firm, I. M. Pei and Associates. It became known in 1966 as I. M. Pei and Partners. The company name would change again in 1989 to become known as Pei Cobb Freed and Partners.

I. M. Pei: Architect

MAJOR PROJECTS

From the start, I. M. Pei was acclaimed for his work. While with Webb and Knapp, he gained national attention for his design of the Mile High Center (1956), in Denver, Colorado. The Mile High Center was one of the first architectural projects joining public space—a pedestrian area with trees, seating, pools, and fountains—with commercial buildings.

Pei served as a lead designer on various projects during the 1960s. According to the Pei Cobb Freed and Partners Web site, the design for the National Center for Atmospheric Research (1967), in Boulder, Colorado, was inspired by cliff dwellings of Mesa Verde Indians of southwestern Colorado. In 1969, the American Institute of Architects honored the three-story Everson Museum of Art, in Syracuse, New York.

One of the better-known projects of the 1970s was the presidential library and museum facility in Boston, Massachusetts—the John F. Kennedy Presidential Library (1979). Another I. M. Pei project completed during the 1970s is the National Gallery

The John F. Kennedy Presidential Library, designed by I. M. Pei, contains historical materials covering the administration of the 35th president of the United States.

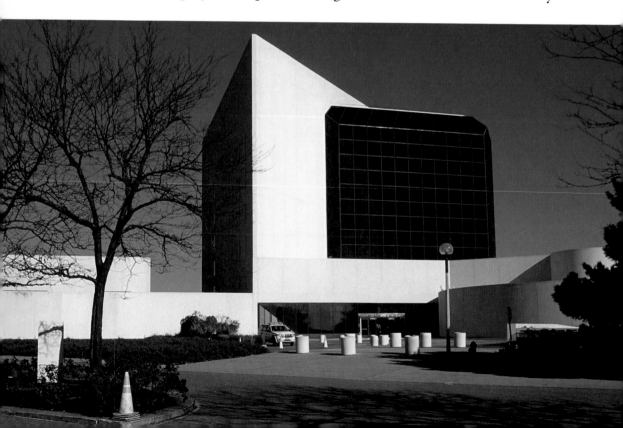

of Art, East Building, located in Washington, D.C. (1968–78). The wing is widely rated as one of Pei's most important buildings, and the design won several national awards.

One of I. M. Pei's most striking, and somewhat controversial buildings, is the 1981 glass pyramid that serves as an entrance to the Louvre Museum in Paris. At first many Parisians thought the ancient pyramidal structure did not fit in with the stately former 12th-century palace. But eventually the entrance became accepted as well as admired.

"Architecture," Pei has said, in discussing the essence of the profession, "really is the need to synthesize the best out of life, out of history. Whatever is still valid, I do not care how old it is, use it."

As the sun sets over the Louvre Museum, in Paris, France, the distinctive pyramidal entrance designed by I. M. Pei lights up the palatial surroundings.

I. M. Pei: Architect

AWARD-WINNING ARCHITECT

Through the years, Pei was been honored many times. In 1975 he was elected to the American Academy of Arts and Sciences. Three years later he became chancellor of this nationally prestigious group, and the first architect to be honored with this position. Another honor came in 1979 when Pei received the Gold Medal from the American Institute of Architects, the Institute's highest award.

A crowning honor came with the International Pritzker Architectural Prize in 1983. Often described as architecture's most prestigious award, it is given annually to a living architect. Named for the Pritzker family, the prize recognizes people who have made significant contributions through the art of architecture. When he accepted the award at a June 1983 ceremony, Pei acknowledged that many people have helped ensure his success. He explained:

> The practice of architecture is a collective enterprise, with many individuals of various disciplines and talents working closely together. And from the commissioning to the completion of a project, there are also the many individuals for whom architects work, whose contribution to quality is frequently as crucial as that of the architect. So I accept this prize for all who have worked with me in this unique undertaking.

The International Pritzker Architectural Prize includes a $100,000 grant. Pei used the money to fund a scholarship program for Chinese students to study architecture in the United States.

Many other awards and honorary doctorates, both within the United States

◀ **CROSS-CURRENTS** ▶

In the late 1980s I. M. Pei was offered the commission to design the Rock and Roll Hall of Fame, located in Cleveland, Ohio. To learn more, turn to page 52.

and from foreign countries, have come to Pei throughout his long career. He has said that one of the most significant was the Medal of Liberty, bestowed by President Ronald Reagan on July 4, 1986. It was shared with 11 other naturalized citizens of the United States who, on the occasion of the 100th birthday of the Statue of Liberty, were being honored for their contributions.

Although Pei officially retired from his firm in 1990, he continues to maintain a small office in New York City, where he and his wife live. The Peis have three sons and one daughter. Two sons, Chien Chung "Didi" Pei and Li Chung "Sandi" Pei have become architects themselves.

CHAPTER THREE

Daniel C. Tsui: Physicist

Chinese-born Daniel Tsui has contributed much to the study of physics during his life in the United States. In his research Tsui has made significant discoveries related to the electrical properties of thin films and microstructures of semiconductors.

EARLY YEARS

Daniel C. Tsui was born on February 28, 1939, to a poor farming family living in a village in the province of Henan, located in central China. His parents were illiterate, but they wanted their son to receive a good education. In 1951, at the age of 12, Daniel was sent to live with two older sisters in Hong Kong. He never saw his parents again.

In Hong Kong Daniel had to learn to speak the Cantonese dialect, which was different from the language spoken in his village. However he thrived at Pui Ching Middle School, the Baptist secondary school he attended. Starting at the sixth grade level he showed great promise in science.

After graduating in 1957 Tsui traveled to the United States to attend his church pastor's alma mater, Augustana College. Daniel had received a full scholarship at the school, which is located in Rock Island, Illinois.

CONTINUING EDUCATION

Well-liked by his college classmates, Tsui was elected "Mr. Friendship" by fellow students in his senior year. He excelled in science at Augustana College, graduating with Phi Beta Kappa honors and a bachelor's degree in 1961.

Tsui went on to graduate school at the University of Chicago, where he secured a position as a research assistant for solid-state physicist Royal Stark. Tsui explained the direction of his research: "I realized quite early that I wanted to do experimental physics and that I lacked the aptitude for colossal experimental setups and also the taste for grandeur. I wanted to do table-top experiments and be allowed to tinker."

An early interest in science led to a career in physics research for Daniel C. Tsui, who poses in this April 1998 photograph in his laboratory at Princeton University, New Jersey.

Daniel C. Tsui: Physicist

Tsui's research often required monitoring experiments 16 to 18 hours a day, seven days a week. Despite the time commitment, while working at the University of Chicago, Tsui met and fell in love with undergraduate student Linda Varland. They were married after her graduation, in 1964. Tsui obtained his Ph.D. in physics in 1967.

NEW FRONTIER IN PHYSICS

Tsui continued his research in solid-state physics, focusing on semiconductor research in 1968. In the spring of that year he left the academic world to work for Bell Laboratories in Murray Hill, New Jersey, working in the Solid State Electronics Research Laboratory. He would later describe his work in disorder and electron-electron interaction as "a new frontier." It would also be referred to as "two-dimensional electron physics."

Daniel Tsui holds a computer drawing that illustrates his Nobel Prize–winning discovery of the fractional quantum Hall effect.

Working with Tsui at the Bell Labs were two other scientists—Horst L. Störmer and Robert B. Laughlin, and together the three men made a significant discovery in physics. They determined that electrons in a powerful magnetic field at very low temperatures can form a quantum fluid whose particles have fractional electric charges. This effect is known as the fractional quantum Hall effect.

Shortly after that discovery, Tsui moved to Princeton University, in New Jersey, in February 1982. He had decided to become a teacher, and had joined the university's department of electrical engineering as a professor. At the same time he continued his research in solid-state physics.

RECOGNITION AND AWARDS

As a result of his discovery Tsui received the Oliver E. Buckley Condensed Matter Prize from the American Physical Society, awarded in 1984. In 1987 he was elected to the National Academy of Sciences, an honorific society that recognizes distinguished achievement in research in science and engineering. And in April 1998 he was awarded the Benjamin Franklin Medal in Physics, which honors those who have made significant contributions to science and technology.

International recognition came later that year. On October 13, 1998, the Royal Swedish Academy of Sciences announced that Daniel C. Tsui, along with Horst L. Störmer and Robert B. Laughlin, would receive the Nobel Prize in Physics. The academy considered the men's discovery a breakthrough in the understanding of quantum physics. The honor was given on December 10 that year in a ceremony held in Stockholm, Sweden.

◀ CROSS-CURRENTS ▶

To learn more about the Nobel Prize in Physics and the names of other Chinese Americans who have received this coveted award, turn to page 53.

Throughout his career Tsui has shown a preference for work in the laboratory and has not sought the spotlight for his many accomplishments. For example, when he found out through a radio news program that he had been awarded the Nobel Prize, he simply went on with his usual weekday morning routine by going to the laboratory.

A LIFE OF LEARNING

When asked whether he has interests other than physics, Tsui has mentioned music. But he says, "I am very interested in music but I have no talent. I have never had time for anything else but physics and have never done anything worth mentioning outside physics."

Teaching, however, is a big part of his life. Tsui once explained that many of his friends and colleagues had questioned why he chose to leave his job with Bell Laboratories in 1982. They wondered why he would leave a life of pure research to become a teacher at Princeton. In response, he referred to the great Chinese philosopher, Confucius, saying:

> Even today, I do not know the answer. Was it to do with the schooling I missed in my childhood days? Maybe. Perhaps it was the Confucius in me, the faint voice I often heard when I was alone, that the only meaningful life is a life of learning. What better way is there to learn than through teaching.

CHAPTER FOUR

Laurence Yep: Storyteller

Chinese-American author Laurence Yep is best known for his books for children and young adults that provide realistic portraits of Chinese-American life in U.S. society. He has published more than 60 books, many of which center on Chinese legends, folk tales, and experiences related by his Chinese family and relatives.

THE OUTSIDER

Laurence Michael Yep was born in San Francisco on June 14, 1948, the younger son of Thomas Gim Yep and Franche Lee Yep. Laurence's mother had been born in the United States of Chinese parents, while his father had come to California from China. The Yep family lived in an apartment over their small, corner grocery store, which was located in a predominately black neighborhood. Both he and his older brother, Thomas, helped out at the store.

During elementary and middle school, Laurence commuted to a bilingual school in Chinatown. There, Yep attended a Catholic high school, where his friends spoke Chinese. But he did not know the language because his parents didn't speak Chinese at home. "I was the Chinese American raised in a black neighborhood, a child who had been too American to fit into Chinatown and too Chinese to fit in elsewhere," Yep would later write in his autobiography, *The Lost Garden*.

As he struggled to realize his own identity, Yep discovered that he could find one through his writing. He has said, "In a sense I have no one culture

Born and raised in San Francisco, California, Laurence Yep is the award-winning author of more than 60 books for young people.

to call my own since I exist peripherally in several. However, in my writing I can create my own [culture]." Many of Yep's works place his main characters in situations as outsiders. The situations typically recall his own experiences of feeling isolated.

BECOMING A WRITER

Yep was encouraged to write by one of his teachers in high school, who challenged him to submit his short stories for publication by a national magazine. At age 18, while a first-year student at Marquette University in Milwaukee, he sold his first story, "The Selchey Kids," to *If* magazine, a science fiction magazine. He was paid a penny per word for his work.

Yep studied at Marquette University for two years. There, he became good friends with Joanne Ryder, the editor of the school's literary magazine. They would stay in touch as he went on to complete his bachelor's degree at the University of California at Santa Cruz, in 1970.

Ryder was working as an editor in the children's books department of the publishing house Harper and Row, in New York City, when she suggested that Yep submit a book for publication. In 1973 Harper and Row published his first novel, *Sweetwater*, which is a science fiction tale about a man from Earth going to a star in space as a colonist. In the meantime, Yep was working on finishing his Ph.D. in English, which he received from the State University of New York in Buffalo in 1975.

Laurence Yep and Joann Ryder would remain in contact over the years. Eventually the two good friends fell in love and in 1985 they married.

A WRITER AND AN OBSERVER

The same year he received his Ph.D., Yep published *Dragon-wings*, a story set in the first years of the 20th century. It is about a young Chinese boy who immigrates to the United States, joining his father in San Francisco, California. The two work together to help the father achieve his dream of building a flying machine. At the same time they deal with the challenges of being outsiders in U.S. society and surviving the San Francisco earthquake of 1906.

Dragonwings, a combination of historical fiction and fantasy, was the first book of what would become the nine-volume Golden Mountain Chronicles. The series tells the stories of seven generations of a fictional Chinese family, covering the years from 1849 to 1995. While fictional, the novels use some material from the Yep family history. The series also includes *The Serpent's Children, Dragon's Gate, The Traitor, Child of the Owl, Sea Glass*, and *Thief of Hearts*.

In a 2002 interview, Yep explained how his Chinese heritage is a part of his writing:

> [I]n my early twenties, I became very interested in my Chinese roots. For years after that, I thought that my function as a Chinese-American writer was to act as a bridge between two cultures. Now, though, I am not so sure that it is possible to blend two cultures together. . . . The two . . . pull in opposite directions. So I see myself now as someone who will always be on the border between two cultures. That works to my benefit as a writer because not quite fitting in helps me be a better observer.

Yep also employs fantasy in some of his tales. His *Dragon* series, for example, is based on Chinese mythology. The first book of the series is *Dragon of the Lost Sea*. That fantasy adventure was followed by *Dragon Steel, Dragon Cauldron*, and

DRAGONWINGS
by Laurence Yep

The 1975 historical novel Dragonwings *was Yep's first book to deal with the Chinese-American experience. It would receive one of publishing's biggest awards in American literature for children—recognition as a Newbery Honor Book.*

Dragon War. The Tiger's Apprentice series is a magical fantasy trilogy consisting of *The Tiger's Apprentice, Tiger's Blood,* and *Tiger Magic.*

Chinese culture, Chinese Americans, and Chinatown are also essential to other books written by Yep. They include several titles in the *Chinatown Mystery* series and *The Rainbow People,* in which Yep retells various Chinese folktales.

AWARD-WINNING WORK

Two of Laurence Yep's novels, both from the Golden Mountain Chronicles, received recognition as Newbery Medal Honor Books. The citation, given by the American Library Association (ALA), was awarded to *Dragonwings* in 1976 and to *Dragon's Gate* in 1994. *Dragonwings* also won several other awards, including the International Reading Association Award, the Friend of Children and Literature Award, and the Phoenix Award. In 1990 Yep won a National Endowment for the Arts literature fellowship.

In 2005 Laurence Yep was awarded the Laura Ingalls Wilder Medal, given every two years by the ALA for substantial and lasting contributions to children's literature. In his acceptance speech for this lifetime achievement award, Yep noted:

> America changed the first Chinese who came here as much as they changed their new country; and America has continued transforming their descendants in ways that I'm still trying to comprehend.

For more than 30 years Yep has been a full-time writer, although he has also taught creative writing and Asian-American studies at the University of California at Berkeley, and at the University of Santa Barbara. He lives near San Francisco with his wife, Joanne Ryder, who is also a children's book writer. At home he and Joanne have separate studies where they write, though they often share thoughts and ideas on their projects.

◀ CROSS-CURRENTS ▶

In much of his writing Laurence Yep describes the actual experiences of Chinese immigrants. For more information, see "Voices from the Past," on page 53.

CHAPTER FIVE

Amy Tan: Author

The daughter of Chinese immigrants, Amy Tan is a major American writer. Much of her work reflects her Chinese heritage and issues that arise among first-generation immigrants and their children, specifically between mothers and daughters. Tan's books have been translated into 35 languages.

LIVING IN TWO WORLDS

Amy Ruth Tan was born on February 19, 1952, in Oakland, California. In Chinese, her name is An-mei, which means "blessed from America." She had an older brother, Peter, born in 1950, and would soon have a younger brother, John, born in 1954.

Amy's father, John, was an electrical engineer and Baptist minister who came to the United States in 1947. Her mother, Daisy, was a vocational nurse who immigrated to the United States in 1949 to escape the political upheaval of the Chinese civil war.

At home Daisy Tan spoke to her children in Mandarin or a combination of Chinese and English—she never learned fluent English. Amy would respond in English—she did not speak Mandarin herself. At school she was the only Chinese-American student in her classes, which led to feelings of isolation. She looked for ways to look, act, and feel American, which often caused conflicts with her mother. An immigrant from China, Amy's mother was very traditional, while Amy, like many Chinese-American youths born in the United States, struggled with her cultural identity.

DEALING WITH TRAGEDY

In 1967 Amy's older brother, Peter, died of a brain tumor. The following year, John Tan also died of a brain tumor. To escape from what she considered a "diseased" house, Daisy moved her remaining children, Amy and John, to Europe later that year.

The family eventually settled in Montreux, Switzerland, where 16-year-old Amy finished high school, graduating from the Monte Rosa Institute in 1968. While they lived in Switzerland, Amy and her mother struggled with their relationship as the daughter rebelled against her mother's attempts to control her.

Author Amy Tan is the daughter of Chinese immigrants who came to the United States in the late 1940s.

A COLLEGE EDUCATION

After graduation Amy followed her mother's wishes by attending the college Daisy had chosen for her—Linfield College, in McMinnville, Oregon. And Amy enrolled as a premed student, as her mother wished.

But for Amy writing was still her major interest. She soon transferred to San Jose State University, in San Jose, California. There she earned a bachelor of arts in English, in 1972, and a master of arts in linguistics, in 1974. While at Linfield, Amy met her future husband, Louis DeMattei, on a blind date. They fell in love and four years later, on April 6, 1974, they married.

WORKING AS A WRITER

By 1983 Amy had become a freelance technical writer, turning out work for business clients in San Francisco. The work, which involved writing training manuals, business reports, and speeches for clients such as AT&T and Apple Computer, paid very well.

Tan promotes her new novel, Saving Fish from Drowning, *at a New York City bookstore in 2005.*

But Amy was dissatisfied with life as a technical writer. She decided to try fiction writing. One of her short story efforts, "Endgame," earned her a spot with a fiction writers workshop group. Written in 1985, the story tells of the conflict between a young Chinese-American girl and her Chinese-born mother. After it was published in *Seventeen Magazine*, Amy submitted it to a literary agent as part of a book proposal for a collection of short stories. Then, in 1987, she and her mother left for a trip to China.

Amy had decided to journey to the land of her parents' birth after Daisy Tan had been hospitalized with severe chest pains. The incident made Amy realize that when her mother died, the story of her past would be lost. Amy was especially interested in finding out more about her mother's life in China before Daisy had immigrated to the United States.

After returning from her travels, Amy learned that a publishing house had accepted her book proposal. Using her mother's stories and her trip to China for inspiration, she wrote *The Joy Luck Club*. Published in 1989, the book is dedicated to Amy's mother. Writing fiction, Amy has said, has helped her to fully understand and appreciate her Chinese heritage.

The Joy Luck Club, which explores the relationships among four Chinese mothers and their Chinese-American daughters, won critical and financial success. The novel was nominated for a National Book Award and Los Angeles Times Book Award. Its paperback rights were sold to Vintage Books for $1.2 million.

OTHER WORK

Daisy Tan's stories helped shape Amy's second book, *The Kitchen God's Wife*, published in 1991. It is based on her mother's experiences as a young girl and woman in 1940s war-torn China. She had been previously married and had children living in China—Amy met her two half-sisters for the first time during her travels to China in 1987.

Later novels by Amy Tan include *The Hundred Secret Senses* (1995), *The Bonesetter's Daughter* (2001), and *Saving Fish from Drowning* (2005). They have been award-winning best-sellers as well. In addition, Amy has written the children's books *The Moon Lady* (1992) and *The Chinese Siamese Cat* (1994). The latter book was used as the basis for a children's cartoon series for PBS entitled *Sagwa*.

In 2003 Tan also published a collection of essays, speeches, and articles entitled *The Opposite Of Fate: A Book of Musings*, which was released in paperback with the subtitle *Memories of a Writing Life*. In that book, she discusses the impact of good fiction, saying,

> ◀ **CROSS-CURRENTS** ▶
>
> In one of her essays, Amy Tan says she writes with an understanding of how difficult communication can be between immigrants and their children. See "Four Different Kinds of English" on page 54.

> It can enlarge us by helping us notice small details in life. It can remind us to distrust absolute truths, to dismiss clichés . . . to see the world freshly from closer up or farther away. . . .
>
> The best stories do change us. They help us live interesting lives.

PERSONAL LIFE

Amy and her husband of more than 30 years, Lou, have homes in San Francisco and in New York City. A favorite form of exercise for Amy—hiking in the countryside outside these cities—led to a serious illness for the author. In 1999 she was diagnosed with Lyme disease, which is caused by a tick bite. By the time the

Amy performs with other authors in a band known as the Rock Bottom Remainders at Chicago's House of Blues, in 2004.

illness was diagnosed, it had caused seriously debilitating symptoms. Subsequently, Amy has pushed for Lyme disease research and helped support LymeAir4Kids. This fund, administered by the Lyme Disease Association, helps families get professional evaluations for children with the disease.

Amy also is a member of a band that performs concerts to raise money for various charities. Called the Rock Bottom Remainders, the makeshift amateur jazz band is made up of writers, including Stephen King, Dave Barry, and Scott Turow. Proceeds from tours have gone to support children's literacy programs.

CHAPTER SIX

Elaine Chao: U.S. Secretary of Labor

Taiwan-born Elaine Chao has served the public for many years in both government and humanitarian agency positions. On January 29, 2001, she was unanimously confirmed by the U.S. Congress to serve as secretary of labor in the cabinet of President George W. Bush. That appointment, as the nation's 24th secretary of labor, made Chao the first Asian-American woman in U.S. history to serve as a cabinet member.

EARLY YEARS AND EDUCATION

Chao Hsiao-lan "Elaine" Chao was born on March 26, 1953, in Taipei, Taiwan, to James S. C. Chao and Ruth Mu-lan Chu. Both had fled to Taiwan from mainland China after the Communist government took control of mainland China in 1949.

In the late 1950s James Chao was sponsored by the Taiwanese government to study in the United States. But he had to leave his wife and two children behind. After living alone for three years in the United States, he was able to send for his family.

In 1961, when Elaine was eight years old, she came to the United States, accompanied by her mother and younger sister. Years later, in an interview with

In January 2001 Elaine Chao, who immigrated to the United States when she was eight years old, became the United State's 24th secretary of labor.

the Wall Street Journal, Chao explained the difficulty of making the month-long journey by cargo ship from Taiwan:

> My sister fell ill during the ocean journey. Seventeen hundred nautical miles, there were no doctors on board and my mother sat up for three nights and three days, just continuously soaking my sister's body, little body, with cold water [to break her fever].

After the long, hard journey, Elaine, her mother, and sister settled in Jamaica, Queens, in Long Island, New York. James Chao eventually founded a ship brokerage and agency business in New York called Foremost Maritime Corporation.

When she first came to New York, Elaine did not speak any English. But she has explained that she quickly learned by copying everything she heard into her notebook. After graduating from Syosset High School in 1971, Chao went on to Mount Holyoke College, a liberal arts women's college located in South Hadley, Massachusetts. Chao graduated in 1975 from the school with a bachelor of arts in economics. In 1979 she received a master's degree in business administration from Harvard Business School, in Boston.

◄ CROSS-CURRENTS ►

Elaine Chao has often talked about what the United States represented for her immigrant parents and what the country represents for other immigrants today. To learn more, see page 54.

WORK EXPERIENCE

After working for the New York City-based banking company Citicorp for a few years, Chao took her first position with the government. In 1983 she became a White House fellow, working for President Ronald Reagan's administration. Her job was in the office of policy development, where she specialized in transportation and trade issues.

The following year Chao moved to the West Coast, where she worked as a vice president for syndications for the BankAmerica Capital Markets Group. In 1986, she returned to Washington.

Transportation Secretary Elizabeth Dole, who knew Chao from her time as a White House fellow, had recruited her for the job of deputy administrator of the U.S. Maritime Administration (MARAD), which is part of the Department of Transportation. MARAD maintains the National Defense Reserve Fleet—ships kept available for national defense or in case of a national emergency. The government agency had been losing $1.6 billion a year. Chao was chosen to administer it because of her experience with shipping, banking, and credits.

As her abilities were recognized, Chao advanced quickly in her professional career. In 1988 she was named chairman of the Federal Maritime Commission. The following year she was named Deputy Secretary of Transportation, becoming the highest-ranking Asian American ever appointed to an executive branch position.

Elaine Chao poses with her husband, Kentucky senator Mitch McConnell. The two were married in 1993.

From 1991 to 1992 Chao served as Peace Corps director during the administration of President George H. W. Bush. The Peace Corps is an independent federal agency that organizes volunteers who work in education, health, and other areas to help improve the quality of life for people in other countries. During Chao's tenure she oversaw the establishment of Peace

Corps programs in several eastern European countries, including Latvia, Lithuania, Estonia, and Poland.

From 1992 to 1996 Chao worked as president and chief executive officer (CEO) of the United Way of America. This nonprofit organization, based in Alexandria, Virginia, is a coalition of charitable organizations that work within communities. Chao assumed leadership of the national organization shortly after its former CEO was convicted of defrauding the organization out of hundreds of thousands of dollars. Chao would be credited with helping restore public trust and confidence in the scandal-ridden organization.

In 1996 Chao went to work as a distinguished fellow at a conservative think tank, the Heritage Foundation. Based in Washington, D.C., the foundation works to establish or promote conservative U.S. government economic and foreign policies.

Through the years, Chao also sat on the boards of several corporations. They include the Clorox Company, Northwest Airlines, and Dole Food Company.

24TH U.S SECRETARY OF LABOR

At the beginning of 2001, Chao took on a new role as head of the U.S. Department of Labor. This section of the executive branch of government is responsible for ensuring the health, safety, retirement security, and competitiveness of the nation's workforce. As secretary of labor, Chao has made many changes within the department that are based on the conservative principles in which she believes.

Some business leaders have praised Chao for her efforts to reduce the complex and sometimes confusing federal regulations that affect industry. In response, she has said, "We in government have a responsibility for ensuring that the regulations that we issue are clear and understandable." Chao has also been praised for bringing greater fiscal management to the department. Supporters cite the fact that the department's budget in

President George W. Bush announced in January 2001 that he was nominating Elaine Chao to join his cabinet as secretary of labor.

2007 was smaller than it had been in 2001, during her first year in charge. At the same time, they note that 2007 workplace injuries were at all-time lows.

However, critics say some of Chao's policies have hurt the common worker. For example, some people say the labor secretary has been responsible for reducing the effectiveness of vital mine safety protections. Others have accused her of collaborating with big business interests at the expense of workers and their unions. Some organized labor groups have complained that under her watch the Department of Labor has imposed unnecessary reforms. Chao's supporters counter that such requirements were long overdue.

Chao has responded to criticisms by saying that she works not just for unionized workers but for *all* workers. She has pointed out that the majority of workers do not belong to a union and that she wants to work with everyone. "I am not pro-business or pro-union," she has said. "I'm pro-worker. I'm for the 11 percent [of workers] who are organized and the 89 percent who are not."

CHAPTER SEVEN

Yo-Yo Ma: Musician

Yo-Yo Ma is one of the world's most accomplished musicians. The renowned cellist has played with major orchestras and in small ensembles at performances held around the world. His many albums demonstrate his extraordinary musical virtuosity and range.

CHILD PRODIGY

Yo-Yo Ma—*Yo* means "friendship" in Mandarin Chinese—was born in Paris, France, on October 7, 1955. His was a musical family. His mother, Marina (born Ya-Wen Lo), was a mezzo-soprano singer in Hong Kong. His father, Hiao-Tsiun, a former professor of music at Nanjing University in China, was a composer and conductor.

In 1936 Hiao-Tsiun emigrated from China to Paris, where he studied at the Paris Conservatoire and earned a doctorate at the Sorbonne. Marina, a former student of Hiao-Tsiun's, immigrated in 1949 to Paris, where they were married. Their daughter, Yeou-Cheng was born in 1951, and Yo-Yo four years later.

As Yo-Yo was growing up, he learned to play the violin, the viola, and the cello under his father's careful instruction. At the age of four, he had to memorize two measures a day of Johann Sebastian Bach's cello suites over the course of six months. At age five he performed at his first public concert at the University of Paris.

When Yo-Yo was seven, his family moved to New York City. In 1963, at age eight, he performed at an American Pageant of the Arts concert on national

A late 1970s photograph of Yo-Yo Ma. His abilities were acknowledged early in his career, when in 1978 he received the Avery Fisher Prize. The award is given to American musicians for outstanding achievement in classical music.

television. And he made his debut recital as a cellist at New York's famous Carnegie Hall, with his sister playing the violin, when he was just nine years old.

A CERTAIN CHARISMA

Ma went on to the renowned Juilliard School of Music in New York, where he studied with American cellist Leonard Rose. His talent, exceptional memory, and virtuosity soon attracted conductors seeking to engage the teenager for concert performances.

After spending a semester at Columbia University, Ma transferred in 1972 to Harvard University. While at Harvard he performed as a soloist with major orchestras, playing at 30 concerts around the world during his freshman year. That schedule proved too difficult and for the remaining three years of college, he limited out-of-town performances to just one per month.

The summer before entering Harvard, 16-year-old Yo-Yo had met Jill Hornor at the Marlboro Festival, in Vermont. The Mount

Holyoke student and violinist was two years older. The two remained in contact by phone and mail. Two years after Yo-Yo graduated from Harvard, on May 20, 1978, they were married.

Ma soon achieved an international reputation as a premier cellist. He was famous not only for his smooth and tonally rich interpretations of classical music, but also for his warm and personable stage personality. A longtime friend of Ma's, violinist Lynn W. Chang, told an interviewer that Yo-Yo Ma is successful because he connects so well with his audience. She says:

> There is a certain personality and persona in his playing—he is just a wonderful communicator. There are many who play their instruments well on stage, but there are a select few who are able to go beyond that—who have a certain charisma that goes over the footlights—that makes the audience fall in love with them.

EXPLORING MUSIC

Ma is particularly acclaimed for his rendition of Bach's *Suites for Unaccompanied Cello*, which he recorded in 1983 and again from 1994 to 1997. The second recordings of Bach's six suites for unaccompanied cello were part of a multimedia experiment in which each of the recorded suites was accompanied by a video of the work of a different artist. In 1999 *Bach Cello Suite #6: Six Gestures* was nominated for a Grammy Award for Best Long Form Music Video.

In his search for understanding what music is, Yo-Yo has moved well beyond classical music to explore the compositions and instruments of people around the world. In the Silk Road Project that

◄ CROSS-CURRENTS ►

The ancient network of trade routes known as the Silk Road allowed for the exchange among various cultures of many things besides goods. To learn more about Yo-Yo Ma's Silk Road Project, turn to page 55.

Yo-Yo Ma: Musician

he founded, he has performed with artists from countries such as Iran, China, and Azerbaijan—which bordered the ancient trade route.

In exploring music, Ma has often woven various genres—bluegrass, jazz and swing, folk, pop, tango, and African music—with classical sounds. The end result is crossover music—or works that appeal to various musical tastes. For example, Ma's popular album *Appalachia Waltz* (1996) brought together folk and classical traditions. It was recorded with Nashville country fiddler Mark O'Connor and bassist Edgar Meyer, of the Lincoln Center chamber Music Society in New York.

Ma's performances have also been featured on film sound-tracks. He has played compositions written by John Williams for *Seven Years in Tibet* (1997) and *Memoirs of a Geisha* (2005), which he performed with violinist Itzhak Perlman. *Memoirs* won a Grammy Award for Best Score Soundtrack Album. Ma is also featured on the soundtrack for the 2000 action film *Crouching Tiger, Hidden Dragon*.

In the course of his career, Ma has produced more than 50 albums. And he has been honored with more than 15 Grammy Awards.

EDUCATING THROUGH MUSIC

Yo-Yo Ma is strongly committed to involving children with music. He participates in the Children's Orchestra Society (COS), which was founded by his father. The organization provides kids with instruction and coaching in music, as well as opportunities to perform with celebrated soloists such as Yo-Yo Ma. COS

Members of the Silk Road Ensemble join Yo-Yo Ma (top left) at radio station KCRW's World Festival, held in August 2005 at the Hollywood Bowl, in Los Angeles, California.

is run by his sister, Yeou-Cheng, and her guitarist husband, Michael Dadap.

When Ma tours, he also teaches master classes to student musicians and participates in other programs to educate people who are not musicians. As CultureConnect Ambassador, a U.S. State Department role given to Ma in 2002, he has introduced and taught music theory to students in countries around the world. In June 2006 he was named a Peace Ambassador by the United Nations.

UNDERSTANDING THE WORLD

Yo-Yo and his wife, Jill, have two children, Nicholas and Emily, and live in the Boston area. The renowned cellist looks back on his own parents as having given him a special understanding of the world because they were immigrants. In an interview, he once said:

> I think one of the best lessons that I received from my parents is to have the ability to understand the world beyond yourself. Since my parents were immigrants, they knew a number of different worlds. There's always an awareness that you're a part of things much bigger than yourself.

CHAPTER EIGHT

Lucy Liu:
Actress

A highly popular and well-known actress in both television and movies, Lucy Liu is the daughter of immigrant parents from Taiwan. *Goldsea Asian American Daily* calls her one of the 100 Most Inspiring Asians of All Time.

EARLY YEARS

Lucy Alexis Liu was born on December 2, 1968. She grew up in the Jackson Heights section of Queens, a borough of New York City. Her father, Tom Liu, was a civil engineer and her mother, Cecilia Liu, was a biochemist. The two met in New York as college students. Lucy is the youngest of three children. She has a brother, John Ya Liu, and a sister, Jenny Liu.

Although living in New York, Lucy learned how to speak Chinese before she spoke English. Her parents spoke Mandarin at home. She did not learn much English until she was about five years old and went to public school. In an interview she talked about how children who do not know English can often feel isolated:

> I grew up speaking Chinese. I think when you grow up Asian-American it's difficult because you don't know if you're Asian or you're American. You get confused, and I think when you speak the language, you just can associate with that culture so much easier and you don't become, "I'm going to dye my hair yellow, and I'm going to put blue contacts in,

Lucy Liu (right) appears with her mother, Cecilia Liu, at the 1999 Emmy Awards in Los Angeles. Liu had been nominated for Best Supporting Actress in a Comedy Series for her role in the television show Ally McBeal.

and I'm going to be somebody that I'm not." And not that there's anything wrong with that. I just think you can assimilate to both and not feel that you're outcast.

FINDING ACTING

After graduating in 1986 from Stuyvesant High School—a New York City public high school that specializes in mathematics and science—Liu went to New York University, in New York City. A year later she transferred to the University of Michigan, in Ann Arbor, where she received a bachelor of science in Asian languages and culture. She also received a great impetus for acting when she was cast in her senior year in the lead role of a college production of *Alice In Wonderland*.

After college Lucy went home to New York and tried to establish an acting career. She went to auditions while supporting herself in jobs as a secretary and an aerobics instructor. She had better luck getting acting jobs after moving to Los Angeles a year later. From 1991 to 1996, Lucy secured guests spots on such television shows as *Beverly Hills 90210*, *L.A. Law*, *Coach*, *Home Improvement*, *ER*, and *The X Files*.

Lucy finally gained national fame, however, after being cast in a major role in the hit television comedy *Ally McBeal*,

◄ CROSS-CURRENTS ►

When she was growing up, Lucy Liu spoke Mandarin Chinese at home. For more information about the growing numbers of people speaking the Chinese language in the United States, turn to page 55.

Lucy (far right) appears with the rest of the cast of Ally McBeal *in this 1998 promotional photograph. Top (left to right): Vonda Shepard, Courtney Thorne-Smith, Gil Bellows, Jane Krakowski, Greg Germann, Portia de Rossi, Peter MacNicol, and Lucy Liu. Sitting: Calista Flockhart (left) and Lisa Nicole Carson.*

which ran from 1997 to 2002. As the ill-tempered, but glamorous attorney Ling Woo, she took on a role that made her famous. Playing that part, she would later say, "really changed my mentality. I just thought, 'Wow, anything is possible.' That's when I started really living my life."

Because of her role in *Ally McBeal*, Lucy was nominated in 1999 for an Emmy for Outstanding Supporting Actress in a Comedy Series. She also received a Screen Actors Guild Award nomination in 2000 for Outstanding Performance by a Female Actor in a Comedy Series.

FILM AND TELEVISION ROLES

Lucy's popularity on television led to film roles, including Mel Gibson's action film *Payback* (1999) and the western *Shanghai Noon* (2000), starring Jackie Chan. A major role in *Charlie's Angels* (2000), in which she costarred with Drew Barrymore and Carmeron Diaz, cemented Liu's stature as an important actress. The Angels reprised their roles in a sequel, *Charlie's Angels: Full Throttle* (2003).

In 2003 Lucy played a part in *Kill Bill.* In order to play the part of a Japanese assassin, Liu had to learn how to use a samurai sword, master the intricacies of kimono arrangements, and study Japanese. For her part in *Kill Bill* she won a MTV Movie Award for Best Movie Villain.

After appearing in 2007 on the ABC comedy-drama *Ugly Betty,* Lucy took on the regular role of Mia Mason, an aggressive magazine publisher, in the television comedy *Cashmere Mafia.* The show is about four female executives who support each other, their careers, and families in New York City.

Additional films have included the crime drama *Lucky Number Slevin* (2006) and the romantic comedy *Watching the Detectives* (2007). In 2008 Liu appeared in the comedy drama *The Year of Getting to Know Us.*

Lucy has also lent her voice to several animated characters. On television, she had a recurring voice role on *Maya and Miguel* (2004) and a guest role on *The Simpsons* (2005). In *Kung Fu Panda* (2008), an animated film about an overweight panda that wants to become a kung fu master, she gives voice to a snake called Master Viper. In another 2008 animated film, *Tinkerbell*, Lucy provides the voice of a fairy called Silvermist.

BRANCHING OUT

In recent years Lucy has also branched out as a film producer. In 2006 she was the executive producer on *Freedom's Fury*, a dramatization of the 1956 Hungarian revolution that was crushed by the Soviet Union. In 2007 she served as executive producer of *Code Name: The Cleaner*, which starred the comedian Cedric the Entertainer and herself.

Actress Lucy Liu poses before some of her artwork at a benefit auction for UNICEF held in September 2006 in New York City.

In addition to a career in show business, Lucy has developed a reputation as a serious painter. She first took up the hobby at age 18, and seven years later received a grant to study art in China. In some of her works, Liu creates a multi-media array by using paint, wood, and paper to create striking visual effects. She has displayed her collages, paintings, and photography at several gallery shows.

REACHING OUT TO HELP OTHERS

The talented artist also lends her time and efforts to help numerous charitable organizations. For example, Lucy donates her share of profits from her art shows to the United Nations Children's Fund (UNICEF). In 2005 UNICEF named Liu a Celebrity Goodwill Ambassador for the organization. That position has involved traveling around the world as a spokesperson for efforts that offer global help and health care for underprivileged and needy children. Missions have taken Lucy to troubled areas of Pakistan, in Asia, and to Lesotho and the Democratic Republic of the Congo, in Africa. She once visited six countries in nine days as part of a UNICEF mission.

Lucy provides academic sponsorship to a Lesotho orphan and a South African medical student. She explains her motivation by saying, "It's like making contact with the other side of the world that is now part of my heart and my family."

ATTITUDES TOWARD IMMIGRATION

The Gallup organization surveys people around the world to determine public opinion regarding various political, social, and economic issues. One issue that Gallup has researched over the years is immigration to the United States. In general, Americans have a positive view of immigration, reports the Gallup Web site:

Three in four [Americans] have consistently said it has been good for the United States in the past, and a majority says it is good for the nation today. However, Americans still seem interested in limiting the amount of immigration.

When asked in a July 2008 Gallup survey about the level of immigration into the United States, 39 percent of Americans favored decreasing the number of immigrants allowed into the country, a decrease from 45 percent a year earlier. However, only 18 percent believe it should be increased.

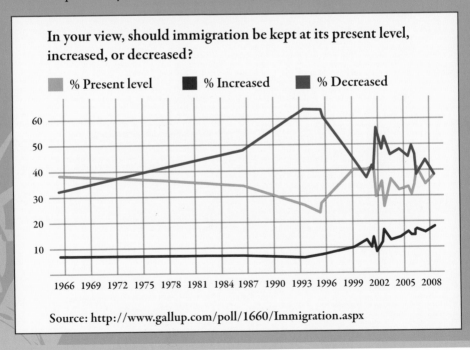

In your view, should immigration be kept at its present level, increased, or decreased?

% Present level   % Increased   % Decreased

Source: http://www.gallup.com/poll/1660/Immigration.aspx

ROCK AND ROLL HALL OF FAME

In 1987 I. M. Pei was offered the commission for designing a new museum in Cleveland, Ohio. The Rock and Roll Hall of Fame would honor musicians, bands, music producers, and songwriters. Because he was unfamiliar with rock and roll music, Pei would later say that he did not believe he was qualified for the assignment. He wrote:

> When the committee from the Rock and Roll Hall of Fame Foundation came and asked me to design the building, I was taken aback. I told them, "You know, I'm not a fan. I'm really not." When I thought of rock and roll, all I thought of was my kids, and with me it was always, "Kids, turn it down. Turn it *down*." But the people on the committee said that it didn't matter than I wasn't yet a fan, and I was greatly encouraged. And so I started my musical education.

Part of this period of instruction involved attending rock and roll concerts and listening to tapes of the Grateful Dead, Elvis Presley, the Beatles and other famous rock and roll musical groups. Pei ultimately designed a remarkable building, completed and dedicated in September 1995, that features a tower emerging from a glass pyramid. The building is located in downtown Cleveland, on the shores of Lake Erie.

In the Rock and Roll Hall of Fame and Museum, Pei combined squares with soaring metal and glass pyramidal shapes to create the $92 million building.

THE NOBEL PRIZE IN PHYSICS

The Nobel Prize is a prestigious international award given out each year since 1901. Today, there are six categories of achievements: physics, chemistry, physiology or medicine, literature, peace, and economics. The award is named after Alfred Nobel, a Swedish chemist and engineer who was the inventor of dynamite. His will established and funded the process of determining winners and the cash prizes that accompany the medal and personal diploma awards.

Committees of the Royal Swedish Academy of Sciences, an independent scientific organization, determine the winners of the Nobel Prizes in physics and chemistry. Those names are announced in October. The Nobel Foundation in Stockholm, Sweden, administers the award ceremonies that are held each year in Stockholm. The ceremonies, which include a lecture by the Nobel laureates, traditionally take place on December 10, the anniversary of Alfred Nobel's death.

The Nobel Prize in Physics is awarded for pioneering discoveries and for groundbreaking inventions in the field of physics. Other Chinese Americans who have won the prestigious award include Tsung-Dao Lee and Chen Ning Yang, in 1957; Samuel Chao Chung Ting, in 1976; and Steven Chu, in 1997.

VOICES FROM THE PAST

Extensive research has played a big part in Laurence Yep's books. He combs through archives of historical material, old newspapers and magazines, and other sources to find interesting information, especially on little known experiences and achievements of Chinese Americans. This material has served as ideas for books.

In *Dragonwings*, for example, Yep drew upon records of a real Chinese-American aviator named Fung Joe Guey. This adventurous Chinese man, showing incredible ingenuity, built a biplane by hand and actually flew it for 20 minutes over Oakland, which is across the bay from San Francisco. This flight in 1909 took place just six years after the much more famous first flight of the Wright brothers at Kitty Hawk, North Carolina.

Yep's works do not draw only on the Chinese immigrant experience of unknown Chinese-American pioneers like Guey. The author's family background has provided a great deal of material, too. Thomas Yep, Laurence's father, came to the United States as a young boy to live with his father. Yep's mother was a second-generation immigrant, born in Ohio and raised in West Virginia. Laurence typically weaves his novels with stories of the challenges that Yep family members faced: basic survival, assimilation, finding one's identity, and dealing with discrimination.

FOUR DIFFERENT KINDS OF ENGLISH

Acommon theme in Amy Tan's novels is misunderstood communication, especially between Americanized daughters and mothers who are not as fluent in English as their children. In her essay "Mother Tongue," Tan explains that she wrote *The Joy Luck Club* by trying to tell the stories in a way that her mother could understand:

> I began to write stories using all the Englishes I grew up with: the English I spoke to my mother, which for lack of a better term might be described as "simple"; the English she used with me, which for lack of a better term might be described as "broken"; my translation of her Chinese, which could certainly be described as "watered down"; and what I imagined to be her translation of her Chinese if she could speak in perfect English, her internal language, and for that I sought to preserve the essence. . . . I wanted to capture . . . her intent, her passion, her imagery, the rhythms of her speech and the nature of her thoughts. . . .
>
> I knew I had succeeded where it counted when my mother finished reading my book and gave me her verdict: "So easy to read."

A BEACON OF HOPE AND OPPORTUNITY

In March 2007, *Forbes* magazine published the words of many U.S. citizens who try to explain what the American Dream means to them. In the publication, Elaine Chao gave her own definition:

> The American Dream is whatever your heart desires. One of the most impressive things I witness whenever I travel across America is the diversity of dreams realized. The promise of the American Dream is a touchstone value of our country, and it acts as a beacon of hope and opportunity to the rest of the world.

Chao has stated that she believes her story as the child of immigrant parents is proof that the United States is "really a land of meritocracy, where it doesn't matter where you were born, who you know." Speaking of her immigrant parents to an interviewer with *The Wall Street Journal*, she credits them with having the courage to believe in the United States as a place where they could have a better future for themselves as well as for their children:

> How they knew what America stood for, or where America was, is pretty impressive to me— that this young couple with no connections, no financial resources to speak of, would dare to audaciously dream that they could come to America.

SHARING CULTURES THROUGH THE SILK ROAD PROJECT

As founder and artistic director of the Silk Road Project, Ma oversees an ongoing series of concerts and the production of music albums that highlight the music and culture of regions of the Silk Road. Just as the ancient 5,000-mile trade route linked different cultures and peoples of the East and West, the Silk Road Project, founded in 1998, promotes the sharing of ideas, art, and music.

The Silk Road Ensemble consists of approximately 60 internationally renowned musicians, composers, and artists from 20 different countries. Its members perform—often playing traditional instruments—at concerts and festivals throughout the world. These events include both traditional and original music. They also incorporate visual arts, storytelling, and dance.

On the Silk Road Project Web site, Ma explains his purpose:

> In my musical journey I have had the opportunity to learn from a wealth of different musical voices—from the immense compassion and grace of Bach's cello suites, to the ancient Celtic fiddle traditions alive in Appalachia, to the soulful strains of the bandoleon of Argentina's tango cafes. . . .
>
> Through this journey of discovery, the Silk Road Project hopes to plant the seeds of new artistic and cultural growth, and to celebrate living traditions and musical voices throughout the world.

THE CHINESE LANGUAGE IN THE UNITED STATES

According to the U.S. Census 2000 report, Chinese is the third most-spoken language in the United States (English and Spanish are first and second). More than 2 million people living in the country speak some dialect of the language. About 72 percent of them report that they speak English well or very well, while 28 percent say they speak English "not well" or "not at all."

The majority speak Cantonese, which is the dialect used by most early Chinese immigrants (who came from the southern part of mainland China then known as Canton). However, in recent years standard Mandarin, which is the official spoken language in the People's Republic of China and the Republic of China (Taiwan), has become more prevalent. Standard Mandarin is based on the Beijing dialect.

Teaching the Chinese language to American-born children of immigrants has been common for decades within Chinese immigrant communities. This way, parents strive to preserve the cultural heritage of their homeland. However, today, many non-Chinese are seeking to learn Mandarin Chinese as the People's Republic of China becomes a rising global economic and political power.

NOTES

CHAPTER 2

p. 15: "Architecture really is . . ." Michael Cannell, *I. M. Pei: Mandarin of Modernism*, (New York: Carol Southern Books, 1995), 351.

p. 16: "The practice of architecture . . ." "Ieoh Ming Pei: Pritzker Architecture Prize Laureate: 1983," http://www.pritzkerprize.com/pei.htm

CHAPTER 3

p. 19: "I realized quite early . . ." "Daniel C. Tsui: The Nobel Prize in Physics 1998: Autobiography," Nobelprize.org. http://nobelprize.org/nobel_prizes/physics/laureates/1998/tsui-autobio.html

p. 20: "a new frontier" "Daniel C. Tsui: The Nobel Prize in Physics 1998," Nobelprize.org.

p. 21: "I am very interested . . ." Magdolna and István Hargittai, *Candid Science IV: Conversations with Famous Physicists* (London: Imperial College Press, 2004), 625.

p. 22: "Even today, I . . ." "Daniel C. Tsui: The Nobel Prize in Physics 1998," Nobelprize.org.

CHAPTER 4

p. 23: "I was the Chinese American . . ." Laurence Yep, *The Lost Garden* (New York: HarperTrophy, 1996), 91.

p. 23: "In a sense . . ." "Laurence Yep," in *Contemporary Authors Online*, Thomson-Gale, 2007.

p. 25: "[I]n my early twenties, I . . ." Leonard Marcus, "Interview with Laurence Yep," papertigers.org, November 2002. http://www.papertigers.org/interviews/archived_interviews/lyep.html

p. 26: "America changed the . . ." Laurence Yep, "Wilder Medal Acceptance," *The Horn Book Magazine* (July-August 2005), 429.

CHAPTER 5

p. 31: "It can enlarge us by . . ." Amy Tan, *The Opposite of Fate: A Book of Musings* (New York: Putnam, 2003), 354.

CHAPTER 6

p. 34: "My sister fell ill . . ." Brendan Miniter, "Elaine L. Chao: 'I See Opportunities in This Country a Little Differently.'" *Wall Street Journal*, July 12, 2008, A9.

p. 37: "We in government have . . ." Brendan Miniter, "Elaine L. Chao: 'I See Opportunities in This Country a Little Differently.'"

p. 38: "I am not pro-business or . . ." David T. Cook, "Elaine Chao: Excerpts from a Monitor Breakfast on Labor Policy," *The Christian Science Monitor*, May 29, 2003. http://www.csmonitor.com/2003/0529/p25s01-usmb.html

CHAPTER 7

p. 41: "There is a certain personality . . ." Sarah A. Dolgonos and Amit R. Paley, "College Taught Ma to Play His Own Tune," *The Harvard Crimson On-line Edition*, June 5, 2001. http://www.thecrimson.com/article.aspx?ref=104513

p. 44: "I think one of the best lessons. . ." Gerri Hirshey, "We Are the World (Cellist Yo-Yo Ma)" *Parade Magazine*, January 30, 2005.

CHAPTER 8

p. 45: "I grew up speaking Chinese. . . ." Sheila Roberts, "Lucy Liu Interview, CodeName The Cleaner," moviesonline.com. http://www.moviesonline.ca/movienews_10807.html

p. 48: "That really changed . . ." Jennifer Armstrong, "Lucy Liu," *Entertainment Weekly*, Jan. 18, 2008, 18.

p. 50: "It's like making contact . . ." Kwala Mandel, *InStyle*, New York, March 2007, 394.

CROSS-CURRENTS

p. 52: "When the committee . . ." Cannell, *I. M. Pei: Mandarin of Modernism*, 379–80.

p. 54: "I began to write stories . . ." Amy Tan, "Mother Tongue," *The Opposite of Fate*, 278–79.

p. 54: "The American Dream is whatever . . ." David M. Ewalt and Michael Noer, "The American Dream: Opportunity Knocks," *Forbes*. October 9, 2007.

p. 54: "really a land of meritocracy . . ." Miniter, "Elaine L. Chao: 'I See Opportunities in This Country a Little Differently.'"

p. 54: "How they knew what America . . ." Miniter, "Elaine L. Chao: 'I See Opportunities in This Country a Little Differently.'"

p. 55: "In my musical journey I . . ." Yo-Yo Ma, "Silk Road Project: Vision." http://www.silkroad-project.org/about/vision.html

GLOSSARY

alien—a foreign-born resident who has not become a naturalized citizen.

assimilate—to become part of a mainstream society or culture.

bluegrass—a variation of country music with its roots coming from Irish, Scottish, and English traditional tunes.

communist—describing a form of government in which all property and businesses are publicly owned and controlled by the state.

electron—a fundamental unit or building block of matter.

emigrant—a person who moves away from his or her country to settle in another country or region.

Emmy—annual award given by the Academy of Television Arts and Sciences to recognize outstanding achievement in television.

ensemble—a small group of musicians, actors, or dancers who perform together.

Far East—China, Japan, and other countries of eastern Asia.

genre—a type, class, or category of music or literature, based on similarity of style or form.

Grammy—an annual music award given by the National Academy of Recording Arts and Sciences for outstanding achievement in the recording industry.

immigrant—a person who comes to live in a new country or region.

naturalization—process in which a person becomes the citizen of another country.

naturalized citizen—a person who has officially acquired the rights of nationality in a country after being born somewhere else.

poll—survey, often conducted over the phone, in person, or over the Internet in which the public's attitudes toward specific issues are documented.

physics—the principles and physical laws of matter and energy. Its study involves areas such as mechanics, heat, radiation, sound, electricity, magnetism, and the structure of atoms.

semiconductor—a solid substance with electrical conductive properties between those of a conductor (which allows electricity to flow) and those of an insulator (which does not allow electricity to flow through it).

union—a organized association of workers formed to promote their interests and rights.

FURTHER READING

Lee, Erika. *America's Gates: Chinese Immigration During the Exclusion Era (1882–1943).* Chapel Hill: University of North Carolina Press, 2005.

Lim, Su-chen Christine. *Hua Song: Stories of the Chinese Diaspora.* San Francisco, Calif.: Long River Press, 2005.

Shane, C. J., ed. *The Chinese.* San Diego, Calif.: Greenhaven Press, 2004.

Teitelbaum, Michael. *Chinese Immigrants.* New York: Facts on File, 2004.

Wong, Li Keng. *Good Fortune: My Journey to Gold Mountain.* Atlanta, Ga.: Peachtree Publications, 2006.

Yung, Judy. *San Francisco's Chinatown.* Mount Pleasant, S.C.: Arcadia Publishing, 2006.

Yung, Judy; Gordon Chang; and Him Mark Lai, eds. *Chinese American Voices: From the Gold Rush to the Present.* Berkeley, Calif.: University of California Press, 2006.

INTERNET RESOURCES

http://www.aiisf.org/
This Web site gives information on the history of Angel Island Immigration station, which served as a Pacific gateway to the United States. It includes links to additional resources about Chinese immigrant experiences.

http://www.apa.si.edu/ongoldmountain/
The Smithsonian Asian Pacific American Program Web site links to information about the Chinese-American experience, historical information and photographs, and the contributions made by Chinese immigrants to the United States.

http://www.cprr.org/Museum/Chinese.html
The Central Pacific Railroad Photographic History Museum Web page provides information and photographs on the Chinese-American contributions to the building of the first transcontinental railroad.

http://www.gallup.com
The Gallup Organization, an international polling institute, provides insights into social issues, politics, sports, entertainment, the environment, and other facets of life though polls available on its Web site.

http://memory.loc.gov/ammem/award99/cubhtml/themeindex.html
An overview from "The Chinese in California 1850–1925" is a Web site from the American Memory Project of the Library of Congress. It contains links to essays and images related to the Chinese immigrant experience.

http://www.nps.gov/history/history/online_books/5views/5views3.htm
This National Park Service Web site reports on the history of Chinese Americans in California, with detailed information on events from the 1850s until 1943.

OTHER SUCCESSFUL CHINESE AMERICANS

Joyce Chen (1917–1994): Born in Beijing, China, Chen was a well-known businesswoman, restaurateur, and chef. Her best-selling *Joyce Chen Cookbook* led to her hosting a television show in the 1960s called *Joyce Chen Cooks*. As an entrepreneur, Chen also founded food and cookware businesses that bear her name.

Connie Chung (1946–): The daughter of a Taiwanese diplomat, Chung was born in Washington, D.C. The television news journalist has headed national television news shows and won three Emmys.

Hiram Fong (1906–2004): Born in Honolulu, Hawaii, Fong served as U.S. senator from Hawaii from 1959 to 1977. He was influential in making Hawaii a state and as a member of Republican Party served several terms in Congress.

David Ho (1952–): Born in Taiwan and naturalized as a U.S. citizen in 1964, Ho is an acclaimed AIDS researcher. He is the founding scientific director and CEO of the Aaron Diamond AIDS Research Center, a world-renowned biomedical research institute.

James Wong Howe (1899–1976): Born in today's Guangzhou, China, Howe came to the United States in 1904. He became a renowned cinematographer of more than 130 films, and was nominated for 10 Academy Awards for cinematography. He won two Oscars for his camera work for *The Rose Tattoo* in 1955 and *Hud* in 1963.

David Henry Hwang (1957–): Born in Los Angeles, California, Hwang is an accomplished playwright especially noted as the author of the award-winning 1988 play *M. Butterfly*.

For more than 25 years, David Ho has been at the forefront of research to help people suffering from human immunodeficiency virus (HIV) and acquired immune deficiency syndrome (AIDS).

Maxine Hong Kingston (1940–): Born in the United States to emigrants from today's Guangzhou, China, Kingston is a novelist known for her award-winning books *The Woman Warrior* (1976) and *China Men* (1980).

Michelle Kwan (1980–): The daughter of Chinese emigrants from Hong Kong, Michelle Kwan is a championship figure skater who has won five World championships and two Olympic medals. She also serves as a public diplomacy ambassador for the U.S. government.

Bruce Lee (1940–1973): Born in San Francisco but raised in Hong Kong, Lee was a martial artist and actor. After returning to the United States when a teen, he later introduced martial arts cinema to the world in early 1970s films such as *Fists of Fury* and *Enter the Dragon*. He died suddenly at age 33 of cerebral edema.

Maya Ying Lin (1959–): The daughter of Chinese immigrants, Lin is an artist and sculptor best known for designing the Vietnam Veterans Memorial in Washington, D.C.

Chang-Lin Tien (1935–2002): Born in Wuhan, mainland China, Tien moved with his family to Taiwan at the end of the Chinese civil war. Tien came to the United States in 1956 to study engineering. Later he was a professor at the University of California at Berkeley, California. He became the first Asian American to head a major U.S. university when he became chancellor at the school in 1990.

An Wang (1920–1990): Born in Shanghai, China, Wang was a computer engineer and inventor who came to the United States in 1945

The most decorated U.S. figure skater in the sport's history, Michelle Kwan has won nine U.S. championship titles as well as five World championships.

to further his studies. He went on to become a developer of computer technology and founder of the computer company Wang Laboratories.

Vera Wang (1949–): Born in New York City to parents who fled China after World War II, Wang is a renowned fashion designer. She has created wedding gowns and other women's clothing for celebrities. Her brand name can also be found on fragrances, jewelry, home fashions, and china and crystal collections.

Other Successful Chinese Americans

INDEX

Numbers in **bold italics** refer to captions.

Ally McBeal, 47, 48
American Dream, 54
Angel Island immigration
    station, 8–9
attitudes, American
    toward China, 10
    toward immigration, 9, 51

Central Pacific Railroad, 6, *7*
Chang, Lynn, 41
Chao, Elaine
    on the American Dream, 54
    career, *34,* 35–36, 37–38
    distinguished positions,
        36–37
    early years and immigration,
        33–35
    education, 35
    with husband Mitch
        McConnell, *36*
Chao, James, 33, 35
Children's Orchestra Society
    (COS), 43–44
China, civil war in, 9–10
Chinatowns, *4,* 7–8
Chinese Exclusion Acts, 6–7, 9
Chinese language, 45–46, 55
Chu, Ruth Mu-lan, 33
citizenship, 8–9
community associations, 7
Confucius, 22

DeMattei, Louis, 29
discrimination, 6–7
Dragonwings (Yep), 25, *26,*
    53

English language, different
    forms of, 54

fractional quantum Hall
    effect, 20

Golden Mountain Chronicles
    (Yep), 25, 26

Heritage Foundation, 37
Hornor, Jill, 40–41, 44

I. M. Pei and Associates, 13
immigrants
    discrimination faced by,
        6–7
    experiences of, 27, 53
    population of, 5, 6–7
immigration
    American attitudes toward,
        9, 51
    Angel Island immigration
        station, 8–9
    laws, 6–7, 9–11
International Pritzker
    Architectural Prize, 16

John F. Kennedy Presidential
    Library, *14*

Laughlin, Robert, 20, 21
Liu, Cecilia, 45
Liu, Lucy
    acting career, 47–49
    in *Ally McBeal, 47,* 48
    awards, *46,* 48
    charitable causes, *49,* 50
    early years, 45–46
    education, 46
    as film producer, 49
Liu, Tom, 45
Louvre Museum, *15*

Ma, Hiao-Tsiun, 39
Ma, Marina Lo, 39
Ma, Yeou-Cheng, 39, 44
Ma, Yo-Yo
    awards, *40,* 43
    charisma, 41
    as child prodigy, 39–40
    as educator, 43–44
    international leadership
        positions, 44
    performances and recordings,
        41–43, *42*
    with Silk Road Project,
        41–42, *43,* 55
McConnell, Mitch, *36*
Mile High Center, 14

National Center for
    Atmospheric Research, 14
National Gallery of Art,
    14–15

Nobel Prize in Physics, Chinese-American recipients of, 21, 53

Peace Corps, 36–37
Pei, Eileen Loo, 13
Pei, I. M.
    awards, 16–17
    career, 13
    early life, 12
    education, 12–13
    major projects, 14–15, 52
    military research, 13
Pei, Lien Kwun, 12
Pei, Tsuyee, 12
People's Republic of China, 10
population, Chinese-American, 11

railroads, construction of, 6, 7
Rock and Roll Hall of Fame, *52*
Rock Bottom Remainders, *32*

Ryder, Joanne, 24

Saving Fish from Drowning (Tan), *30,* 31
Silk Road Project (Ma), 41–42, *43, 55*
Störmer, Horst, 20, 21
Suites for Unaccompanied Cello (Bach), 41

Tan, Amy
    career, 29–30
    early life and education, 28–29
    journey to China, 30, 31
    Lyme disease, 31–32
    in Rock Bottom Remainders, *32*
    works, 30–31, 54
Tan, Daisy, 28, 29, 30
Tan, John, 28, 29
Tan, Peter, 28, 29
The Joy Luck Club (Tan), 30, 54
The Opposite of Fate (Tan), 31

Tsui, Daniel
    awards, *19,* 21
    early life, 18
    education, 18–19
    research career, 19–20
    teaching career, 21–22

UNICEF, *49,* 50
U.S. Maritime Administration (MARAD), 35–36

Varland, Linda, 20

Weisner Building, I.M. Pei with, *13*

Yep, Franche Lee, 23, 53
Yep, Laurence, *24*
    awards, 26
    Dragonwings, 25, *26,* 53
    early life, 23–24
    education, 24
    research of Chinese American experiences, 25, 53
    works, 24, 25–26
Yep, Thomas Gim, 23, 53

PICTURE CREDITS

ABOUT THE AUTHOR

Jack Adler is a Los Angeles-based writer with 11 nonfiction and fiction books to his credit. Nonfiction titles include *Exploring Historic California, Southern India, The Consumer's Guide to Travel, Splendid Seniors: Great Lives/Great Deeds*, and *Travel Safety* (co-authored). The Library of Congress selected the latter book for translation into Braille. He teaches writing courses at UCLA Extension and the Writer's Digest School.